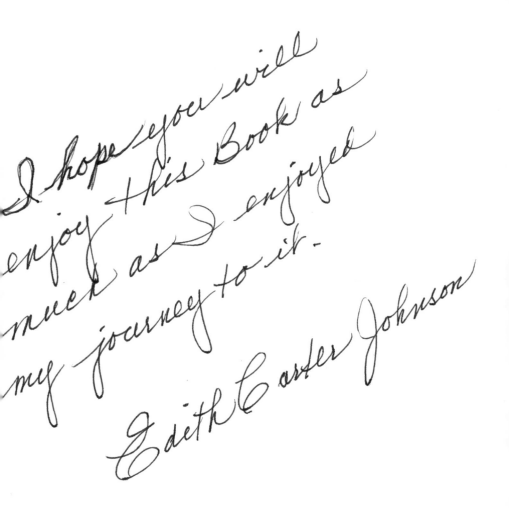

I hope you will enjoy this Book as much as I enjoyed my journey to it —

Edith Carter Johnson

ONLY THE Cash flow IS LOW

Warm and Witty Wisdom...West Indian Style!

EDITH CARTER JOHNSON
illustrated by WILLIAM YANCY COOPER

TATE PUBLISHING
& ENTERPRISES

ISBN: 1–5988634–7–9

DEDICATION

In Loving Memory Of
Kathleen Louise Braithwaite Carter
and
John William Carter

ACKNOWLEDGMENT

Some 35 years ago, my friend, Connie Parham, planted the seed that I should write a book encompassing my Mother's "Sayings" to which I replied, "are you kidding—no way." You see, Connie and my Mother had developed a mutual admiration society and I would share Mother's "Sayings" with her which always resulted in our having a good laugh. So Connie I thank you for being so farsighted.

Of course I must list all of my siblings, including those who are no longer with us -- George, Kathleen, Clarence (Nick), Ottolese, Llewellyn (Lou), Geraldine (Gerri), Mary (Maryce), Mildred, Nathaniel (Nat), Ada, Jean, Charles, and Doris, as their contribution was immeasurable, especially my sister Gerri, who lovingly encouraged me daily through this entire process.

The high-spirited illustrations by the artist, Bill Cooper, and the constant encouragement of Glendora, his wife, made this journey one of my most memorable experiences.

To my very special friends, Brenda Haynes, Patricia Saber, and Noel Mobley, who were with me from day one, assisting and encouraging me in every way they could to bring the book to fruition -- all I can say is that I could not have done it without you.

Finally, believing that God has a plan for each one of us and as we open up ourselves to His will, the possibilities are limitless.

TABLE OF CONTENTS

Foreword 11

Introduction 13

Aim For The Stars Sweetheart, You Can Always Come
    Down A Peg Or Two 15

Believe Me To Father 17

A Belly Full Is A Belly Full 19

They Didn't Even Give Their Mouth Breakfast Time 21

How Do You Know If You Can Win Or Not, You Haven't
    Even Tried 23

Harry Right and Harry Wrong 25

If It's A Minute To Morning You Are Going To Do It 27

Look At My Crosses 29

Only Worry When They Don't Talk About You 31

I'm Going To Ring Your Ear Hole 33

You Know When You Have Clothes Out On The Line–You
    Are Always Looking For Rain 35

I Ain't Able To Laugh 37

I Don't Care If The Teacher Ever Likes You, I Sent You To
    School To Learn 39

Life Is Sweet For Those Who Can Live It 41

Look How Her Face Skin Up 43

Sweetheart If You Want To Keep A Secret Don't Tell Anyone 45

May They Drive You Way Past Your Burying Ground 47

God Never Put A Bird Out There Without A Branch To
    Land On 49

Not A Bit Of Taste 51

Nothing Before Its Time 53

Go Take Your Sunday Clothes Off Your Weekly Skin 55

Hot Needle And Burnt Thread 57

Hurt–You Don't Know What Hurt Is 59

Sweetheart, If You Live Long Enough, You'll Get Old 61

Couldn't Stick A Pin 63

It Pays To Stand On A Corner 65

What The Deuce Are You Talking About? 67

Miss Great Up 69

You Don't Know How Sweet Work Is Until You
        Don't Have It 71

Game Cock Bring Game Hen 73

Go To France 75

So Heavenly Bound That They Are No Earthly Good 77

It Just Went Like Lovely 79

You Have An English Tongue In Your Head–Use It 81

I Sent You To School To Pass–Not Fail 83

She Has On Swan Street Shoes 85

You Just Stand Sticky 87

He's Like A Sly Mongoose 89

You All Go Along 91

True Eye Servant 93

Make Them Come 'Round 95

Just Because You Don't Have Money, You Don't Have To
        Look Like You Don't Have It 97

They Didn't Take It Like It Has Been 99

"Wonna" 101

You Girls Better Find Out What They Do Because I 103
        Know They Do Something 103

Take It With A Grain Of Salt 105

Dead As A Hook 107

A Cover For Every Pot/A Plaster For Every Sore 109

Don't Be Foolish–Do You Think I Would Give You My Last? 111

Beginning Is Half Done 113

Feed Them With A Long Spoon 115

Can You Beat That? 117

God Never Closed A Door That He Didn't Open A Window.... 119

Foolish 'Til Some Left 121

Thanks, But I Didn't Die, He Did 123

Hold The Light For Even The Devil To See 125

I Wondered When You Were Going To Start Using That Bump
   On Your Shoulder.................................... 127

If You Don't Have Horse, You Ride Cow.................... 129

It's Only A Bus Stop On The Way To Where You Are Going 131

It's Not Lost–It's Only Misplaced......................... 133

Jesus, Lover Of My Soul 135

Never Put All Your Eggs In One Basket 137

It's Not How Much Money You Make Sweetheart, It's
   What You Do With What You've Got 139

Full Of Air Sauce And Wind Pudding 141

Haste Makes Waste 143

Too Finey, Finey 145

However You Make Your Bed, You Lie In It 147

Hey, I Fall Off To Nothing 149

God Never Gives You More Than You Can Bear 151

Richness Is Not In Your Pocket It's In Your Thinking.......... 153

She Just Looked Like A Done Out Old Soul 155

The Watched Pot Never Boils............................ 157

If He Knew Better He Would Do Better 159

She Needs Licks 161

Joseph Of Many Colors 163

If You Don't Laugh, You'll Cry 165

I'm Not Ready Yet 167

No Matter How The Corn Sells........................... 169

Oh, For Land Sake 171

Still Pushing 173

To Be Sure 175

You Can Be Still And Make A Big Noise 177

Worry Is Debt Paid Before It Becomes Due 179

Tired . . . I'm Past Tired 181

Two Heads Are Better Than One 183

You Catch More Bees With Honey 185

There Is Nothing Wrong With What You Are Doing,
    The Only Thing That Is Wrong, Is You 187

You Only Pass This Way One Time 189

Free, Single and Disengaged And Not Taking Care Of
    Another Living Soul 191

No True Member 193

Never A Weary Morning 195

If You Think Trying Is Risky Wait 'Til You Get The Bill For
    Not Trying 197

Commencement 199

FOREWORD

This book is delightful! The author has opened up to her readers a treasury of parental sayings that have admittedly enriched her own family life, thirteen brothers and sisters, subsequent generations, and many friends. Her readers will now become the latest beneficiaries of this sparkling collection—one for each year of her Mother's abundant life.

Little did I know that the warm and welcoming embrace by the author's Mother on my first Sunday as the new young priest at St. George the Martyr Church, Toronto, Canada back in 1955 would result in me, my wife Linda, and our four children becoming one extended family with the Carters throughout the fifty years since.

My hope is that you, the reader, will feel personally drawn in by the author's sharing of her Mother's spontaneous utterances, springing from her deeply spiritual resources and delivered in her Barbadian lingo, releasing both to her children and to her ever present Heavenly Father, her love and fun, her wisdom and faith, her compassion and care, her skills and helpfulness.

The author's Father had his own special oral gifts which were philosophical with gently piercing wisdom. She respectfully and thankfully pays tribute to her Father's role which has, for the past forty years, kept her true to her vision and passion expressed through Ego Studios—an environment which has embraced, affirmed, and enriched the lives of thousands in the Buffalo area and beyond, especially the youth, all living testimonies in love and gratitude for her faith and perseverance.

I must emphatically say that the author has been providentially directed in enlisting William Yancy Cooper as the illustrator of each and every saying of her parents. His art gallery is ingenious, yes inspired, as each sketch portrays with humor and color the sayings contained herein and her own precious reflections. The combination of the illustrations and commentaries will help readers to discover, remember, and enjoy the meaning and purpose of their own lives, and the precious occasions and relationships drawn from their own parents and families.

Preparing this Foreword has brought its own rewards to me. May the readers also be open to the spirit and benefits of this unique book.

The Rev. Canon Bill Riesberry

All Saints Day, 2005

INTRODUCTION

As my parents made their way by boat to Halifax, Canada, from their home island of Barbados, British West Indies in 1920, little did they know the wonderful legacy they would be giving to the world–the substance of this book. You see, my Father first left his Island home to work on the Panama Canal and then ventured into Canada to work in the coal mines in Halifax, Nova Scotia. He returned to Barbados for his bride, my Mother, and they were married in Toronto, Canada in 1920.

The next 25 years were spent birthing and raising us, their offspring–fourteen in all, with three dying before their first birthday. We always felt loved and special, not only as a family but as individuals, and even at an early age realized our parents were exceptional. Their love came through their discipline, humor and conversations with us, many of which were relayed via the "sayings" contained in this book, and to this day, my siblings and I rarely have a conversation without one or more of these "sayings" being exchanged. We were always taught to aim high and give life our best, and the word poor was never part of their vocabulary. I never imagined I would be writing this book and that the title would come from one of my Father's favorite "sayings" during my young adult years.

In this year of 2005, with everyone concerned about the importance of "family" and the need to get back to making "family" a priority, I couldn't be more pleased to pass on what was the glue in our wonderful upbringing. It does not mean one escapes the trials life surely will hand you, but it does give one a solid foundation to hold on to and I wanted to share my parents' legacy to us and through us to you.

AIM FOR THE STARS SWEETHEART, YOU CAN ALWAYS COME DOWN A PEG OR TWO

"AIM FOR THE STARS SWEETHEART— YOU CAN ALWAYS COME DOWN A PEG OR TWO" was the best advice my Father gave me many years ago and to this day, I continue aiming for the stars. My Father truly believed that it was a waste of time to aim for something you knew you were capable of attaining. Many times I have become frustrated at the constant reaching for the stars that I would find myself saying in an audible voice, "Thanks a lot, Daddy, now look at the mess I've got myself in." Inevitably, after a period of maybe a week, a month or longer, I would come to my senses a little wiser, and start aiming for the stars once again. It really is the only way to go. Try it—you'll be amazed at how you will soar.

BELIEVE ME TO FATHER

Whenever our Mother would say "BELIEVE ME TO FATHER," we never knew whose "Father" she was referring to, especially when she was very upset over something we did or did not do. We knew she couldn't be talking about her own Father as he had died before she left her home in Barbados, and not our Father, as he was her husband. At that time in our lives it never really mattered, as we knew she had reached her limit. I now know that whenever she said those words she was referring to our Heavenly Father and it was her way of praying for strength to get her through the predicament she was experiencing at that point in time. Sometimes we were lucky and at other times not—but we survived.

A BELLY FULL IS A BELLY FULL

Our Mother loved people and was very social. The fact that she had children did not stop her activities at the Church, Red Cross, Children's Aid Society, Lodge and Social Clubs–after all she had built-in babysitters. Each time she returned home from one of these outings, we would always want to know if and what was served and most of the time our Mother would be very complimentary, but every now and then she would express her dislike by saying, "A BELLY FULL IS A BELLY FULL" and we would always get such a chuckle knowing exactly what she meant. Her bodily animations coupled with her Barbadian accent were worth just hearing her say those words.

THEY DIDN'T EVEN GIVE THEIR MOUTH BREAKFAST TIME

I make no apologies for the fact that I love to talk and nothing feeds me more than a good conversation. Yet, if you saw me with my siblings, you would find that I probably would say the least. It's hard to believe but very true. My siblings and I all live very interesting lives and to this day we thoroughly enjoy the constant chatter of "togetherness." When we were growing up and still living at home, our Mother would always make the comment, "THEY DIDN'T EVEN GIVE THEIR MOUTH BREAKFAST TIME." You should know that we inherited this wonderful ability to express ourselves, from both parents, and to this day none of us would ever be labeled shy. As I grow older, I have learned that it takes a lot of energy–talking that is–and must admit that I find myself being more selective in how I spend my energy knowing that time truly waits for no one.

HOW DO YOU KNOW IF YOU CAN WIN OR NOT, YOU HAVEN'T EVEN TRIED

In life we want guarantees about everything, especially in our young adult years, and if you were as fortunate as I was, my upbringing resulted in my having a strong sense of self. My first experience with self-doubt was in my junior year in high school when I was nominated for President of the Student Council to run against a very popular male student. While being thrilled at this honor, I confessed to my Father that it was really a waste of time to even run, as females are never elected, which was the status quo at that time. My Father, who was the most philosophical and positive person in my life, calmly said, "HOW DO YOU KNOW IF YOU CAN WIN OR NOT, YOU HAVEN'T EVEN TRIED." At that time in my life this simple but profound statement moved me to try and at least give it my best. I did and won and it made the newspapers in our hometown. That experience has never left me, so whenever I find myself in a difficult situation and feel like giving up, I take a deep breath and I just "TRY!"

HARRY RIGHT AND HARRY WRONG

Most siblings while growing up argue and sometimes fight and we certainly did our share. Our Mother would call whoever was involved and we would proceed to shout our version of what happened. Our Mother would say, "Quiet, I'm not interested in hearing about HARRY RIGHT AND HARRY WRONG," as we would both be saying we were "right" and the other one was "wrong." Mother always quickly settled the matter by spanking and punishing us both. As a result of our Mother's handling of sibling rivalries, we learned to get along and to this day we have this great bond we developed and are each other's best friend.

IF IT'S A MINUTE TO MORNING
YOU ARE GOING TO DO IT

You can imagine it would take great organizational skills, a good work ethic, tremendous strength, a lot of love, and a good sense of humor to keep thirteen human beings functioning on a daily level. Our Mother was superb at this. There were before and after school chores, weekend chores, all of which were rotated on a weekly basis. Of course, being children, we procrastinated at times with our chores much to our Mother's dismay resulting in her lamenting to us, "IF IT'S A MINUTE TO MORNING, YOU ARE GOING TO DO IT." Whenever she said this, we knew we could forget about asking if we could do it the next day. At the time, we thought our Mother was being so mean, but today we thank her for the great lesson she taught us for life.

LOOK AT MY CROSSES

As we travel along life's highway, we are bound to run into experiences that have a profound effect on the direction we choose. It does not matter whether these experiences are "positive" or "negative" as they can have a strong affect on our behavior. Whenever my Mother heard something that really struck a nerve, she would often say, "LOOK AT MY CROSSES." I now interpret her use of this phraseology as her way of enlightening us to the fact that in life we will have crosses to bear but the keeping of our faith in God will help us persevere.

ONLY WORRY WHEN THEY DON'T
TALK ABOUT YOU

We all have received criticism that strikes a nerve, and years ago in my early struggles with my business I was upset about this. In discussing it with my Father he smilingly said, "Why are you so upset about what was said? You need to look at it as free publicity for your business, whether the comment is true or not. The only time one should get upset is 'WHEN THEY DON'T TALK ABOUT YOU.' In this way they show they are at least interested and at the same time leaving someone else alone." This made good sense to me and to this day whenever a similar situation arises, I remember my Father's words and experience a great inner peace.

I'M GOING TO RING YOUR EAR
HOLE

When I was in Grades 1 and 2, I had this very bad habit of never waiting for my older brothers or sisters to take me home after school. I would be enjoying my classmates so much that if they invited me to go home with them, I would always go. My Mother was beside herself, as she would then have to send my older brothers or sisters to look for me. The neighborhood I grew up in was one where everybody knew everyone and of course I would easily be rescued. Once found and home, my Mother would lecture to me stating that if I did not listen she would "RING MY EAR HOLE." I, of course, was hardheaded and therefore got my ear hole rung on several occasions until I finally got the message. To this day I do not know why I was so determined not to listen except for the fact that I got special attention from my Mother and must have needed and enjoyed it despite having my "ear hole rung." I still chuckle whenever I think of that time in my life.

YOU KNOW WHEN YOU HAVE CLOTHES OUT ON THE LINE–YOU ARE ALWAYS LOOKING FOR RAIN

There will always be people who seem to enjoy expecting the worse. Being an optimist, at times it is difficult for me to relate to even a small measure of negativity—my belief being that the same energy one gives to "negative" thinking can be given to "positive" with happier results. Most of this thinking I credit to my parents. My Mother often would remark, "YOU KNOW WHEN YOU HAVE CLOTHES OUT ON THE LINE, YOU ARE ALWAYS LOOKING FOR RAIN." In other words, there are some people who are only happy thinking and expecting the worse. The choice is ours.

I AIN'T ABLE TO LAUGH

Have you ever laughed so hard that your insides would hurt? Although painful, it's a wonderful feeling. I can still see and almost hear my Mother laughing so hard that she would say, "I AIN'T ABLE TO LAUGH." Whenever she said this, we would laugh with her and as children would continue to laugh when she wasn't "able." What a great example she left us! Even though she was a tough disciplinarian, when my siblings and I talk about our Mother we always laugh about her laughing—one of the many loving gifts she gave us.

I DON'T CARE IF THE TEACHER EVER LIKES YOU, I SENT YOU TO SCHOOL TO LEARN

My Father never minced words when it came to education, so when my brother, George, came home from school one day complaining about the fact that the teacher didn't like him, my Father's reply was, "I DON'T CARE IF THE TEACHER EVER LIKES YOU, I SENT YOU TO SCHOOL TO LEARN." You can believe that this statement, along with other remarks made to my brother at that point in time, had a positive and profound effect on his life. So much so that my brother became a successful lawyer, husband and father, and is presently enjoying his retirement as a former Judge of the Ontario Court of Justice (formerly the Provincial Criminal Court of Ontario, Canada). Yes, of course our Father never missed an opportunity to repeat these same words to any one of us when the need arose.

LIFE IS SWEET FOR THOSE WHO CAN LIVE IT

Now that life has blessed me with a few wonderful years, I realize that I was given a real "head start" by my first role models—my parents. I can still hear my Mother who would never miss an opportunity to say, regardless of whether anyone was actually listening, "LIFE IS SWEET FOR THOSE WHO CAN LIVE IT" and sweet it was for her. I can't recall anything that my Mother did not enjoy, even when she was scolding us. Her zest for life was contagious—so much so that she was able to give each of her children a healthy dose and still had plenty left over for others. What a light she was, not only to her family, but to everyone who had the privilege of having her cross their path.

LOOK HOW HER FACE SKIN UP

The fact that our Mother was so loving and had a great sense of humor, we never lost sight of the fact that she was a tough disciplinarian. When she was in one of her "you-better-listen-to-me moods," we would start frowning and our Mother would say, "LOOK HOW HER FACE SKIN UP and I haven't even touched her," meaning that we were only receiving the words outlining her punishment and therefore should not be frowning. At times we would have preferred a spanking as it was usually quick and soon forgotten.

SWEETHEART, IF YOU WANT TO KEEP A SECRET—DON'T TELL ANYONE

It has taken me such a long time to totally believe what my Father told me years ago. He would say to me, "SWEETHEART, IF YOU WANT TO KEEP A SECRET, DON'T TELL ANYONE." I truly believe that we are basically trusting human beings and in our desire to share have told some very private things, which may have been better left unsaid. As I develop a closer walk with God, I do not feel the need to share my every thought with anyone, knowing that God already knows what I'm thinking and I just leave it there. Obviously, when my earthly Father was relaying this thought to me, he already knew what I'd just learned.

MAY THEY DRIVE YOU WAY PAST YOUR BURYING GROUND

My Mother was not only a great disciplinarian, but she could put the fear of God in you with some of the remarks she made. Of course with so many children she had rules and regulations for everything. There were grave results when we refused to heed her warnings, but whenever she would use the words, "MAY THEY DRIVE YOU WAY PAST YOUR BURYING GROUND," we knew she was dead serious. Her intention was to scare the living daylights out of us with these words and she did! Just think of the possibility of being in the wrong place at the wrong time with the wrong people, and end up being driven way past your burying ground and never found or heard of again. It gave us a lot to think about.

GOD NEVER PUT A BIRD OUT THERE WITHOUT A BRANCH TO LAND ON

How does one measure faith? I really do not know the answer but the Bible says that with "mustard seed faith" one can move mountains. It has taken me a long time to accept the fact that God truly does a better job of handling my life than I do. With age comes wisdom, hopefully, as I now find myself daily prioritizing my life making sure I take time out for meditation which usually takes place while walking. Further, it makes me aware of what great faith my parents must have had to raise all of us, especially during the depression years. Not only were they concerned about our basic needs, but continuously fed us spiritually with remarks such as the one above. Their constant prayer was that we always put our best foot forward no matter what road we traveled.

NOT A BIT OF TASTE

Our Mother's outspoken honesty always affirmed the fact that this was really her first time here on this earth. Most of you know that on Sunday morning when leaving church, it is customary to shake the Minister's hand. On one such Sunday, our Mother who always gave our Minister a great big hug, said to him, "NOT A BIT OF TASTE." She, of course, was referring to the sermon that morning adding that it was dry. Our Minister affectionately chuckled and promised he would do better the next Sunday. We were in shock, as we could not believe our Mother had said what she did, but on the other hand it was one of our Mother's redeeming qualities—her loving honesty.

NOTHING BEFORE ITS TIME

I think that the initial seed to do this book started some 30 years ago when I was very involved in moving my own business forward. Then, about ten years ago, my siblings and I really got serious about writing down all of the sayings our parents had so richly endowed us with. One of my Mother's favorite sayings, no matter what it was we were anxious about was "NOTHING BEFORE ITS TIME." She said this so often that it got to the point we would refrain from telling Mother many of our growing pains, especially during our teen-age years. Wisdom does or should come with age and experience when we are willing to acknowledge the fact that no matter how much we plot and plan, God has His timetable for our lives and He is always on time.

GO TAKE YOUR SUNDAY CLOTHES OFF YOUR WEEKLY SKIN

Each time I find myself changing into "at home" clothes after returning from Church, work, or a social affair, I salute my Mother. She was adamant about the fact that we change into "play clothes" each day after school. I especially remember her Sunday comment to us after returning home from Church, when she would lovingly but sternly say, "GO TAKE YOUR SUNDAY CLOTHES OFF YOUR WEEKLY SKIN." As a child you never fully realize the impact parents have on your life. My siblings and I often talk about how fortunate and blessed we were to have parents who used their good old-fashion common sense, love and discipline raising us—a crying need in many of today's children.

HOT NEEDLE AND BURNT THREAD

When we were in our teens, two of my sisters and I really got the sewing bug, something we inherited from our Mother. Our big downfall with sewing is that we would always wait until the last minute to make something we knew weeks earlier we were going to need. If you sew you can relate to this. Our Mother would always refer to this effort by us as using a "HOT NEEDLE AND BURNT THREAD." Not only did Mother use these words with us when the results of our efforts were not up to her standard, but would share with us whenever someone told her that they made whatever they were wearing and it did not look that great. We would all chuckle!

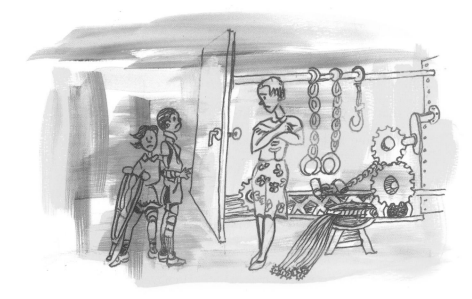

HURT–YOU DON'T KNOW WHAT HURT IS

When you know you have done something you were not supposed to do and especially if it resulted in the policeman bringing you home and ringing your doorbell, you really want to miraculously disappear. This happened to my sister Mary and I after we were in a car accident, even though our Mother had preached to us never to go riding in anyone's car, but being "we are going to do it anyhow" teen-agers, we disobeyed. Further, we never knew anyone who owned a car, and this was exciting! When our Mother answered the door, we knew we were in for it. The policeman was very gracious assuring our Mother we were not hurt too badly, even though my leg was all taped up and I was hurting a lot. Our Mother nodded, thanked the policeman, closed the door and said, "HURT–YOU DON'T KNOW WHAT HURT IS" and proceeded to add her spin to the "hurt" by giving us a spanking to remind us that she was the Mother and we were the children.

SWEETHEART, IF YOU LIVE LONG ENOUGH, YOU'LL GET OLD

As children we can't even visualize getting older. Maybe we express great excitement when we finally reach our teen years especially when we become all of "sixteen" like I did. At this age, we naively think that old age is not even a possibility and we are going to be "forever young." Not so, as in the recesses of my mind I could remember my Father saying to me, "SWEETHEART, IF YOU LIVE LONG ENOUGH, YOU'LL GET OLD." I would privately brush this comment off, as that was the last thing I wanted to hear. Nevertheless, time waits for no one and I now respect his comment, as I'm thankful to be a senior enjoying the journey.

COULDN'T STICK A PIN

Every community has its official mourner and our Mother was high on the Toronto list. I truly believe she enjoyed attending funerals. The fact that she died in her 94th year attests to the fact that she attended a lot of them. Her favorite comment when she returned home from a funeral was "COULDN'T STICK A PIN," which meant there were a lot of people in attendance. She would then elaborate on every detail always reminding us of what kind of funeral she wanted. When it was time for our Mother's "home going," we did exactly what she told us to do. We know she is still on the scene helping direct our path "home."

IT PAYS TO STAND ON A CORNER

My second eldest brother, Clarence, had this wonderful habit that no matter where he saw one of his sisters, he would park his truck, get out, sneak and pick us up, swing us around and give us a big hug. He also would give us a couple of dollars, which back in the 50s, was a lot of money. My Mother got the biggest kick out of this, especially when she would be on the receiving end while waiting for a streetcar or a light to change and my brother would appear out of nowhere. Besides loving to see him so unexpectedly and the fact that he always gave her money, after returning home, Mother would comment with great delight, "IT PAYS TO STAND ON A CORNER" and we would laugh. It was always a "win-win" experience for both of them.

WHAT THE DEUCE ARE YOU TALKING ABOUT?

Growing up I never equated the word "deuce" with a tennis score, but felt that it was a "bad" word and now realize that it was my Mother's way of swearing without really swearing. Neither of my parents ever swore and I still consider swearing a poor excuse to try and get one's point across. I ashamedly admit to using some expletives on very rare occasions, which always left me with a bad feeling and have added this to my "don't do" list. The English language is so beautiful and I smile to myself whenever I remember my Mother's closest brush at swearing was, "WHAT THE DEUCE ARE YOU TALKING ABOUT?"

MISS GREAT UP

If you personally knew me, you would know that my mantra is and always has been "that it is important to truly love yourself," but not to the exclusion of others. When one is comfortable in one's own skin it is much easier to love others and to enjoy your life to the fullest. I have always felt a sadness for people who were so carried away with their own importance that they missed out on life. Whenever this thought crossed my mind I would chuckle remembering my Mother's special name for any one who acted in this fashion—"MISS GREAT UP." Where she got the saying I never knew, but she got great pleasure saying it when the opportunity arose.

YOU DON'T KNOW HOW SWEET WORK IS UNTIL YOU DON'T HAVE IT

The fact that I love to work is due in large measure to my parents and their great example. We were taught at an early age the importance of getting an education so that we could get a decent job and be able to take care of ourselves. My Father would say that he never wanted us to be out of a job to experience, "HOW SWEET WORK IS . . ." due to the fact that we didn't have one. He would always tell us that no matter what type of work we find ourselves in that we always give it our best and would always add that if we were a street-sweeper that we be the best we could be. It really works!

GAME COCK BRING GAME HEN

We all have skeletons in our closets and whenever my Mother would hear us just plain gossiping, she would interrupt and say, "GAME COCK BRING GAME HEN." In other words, while we would be running our mouths about someone, and in some cases not even knowing whether or not it was true, somebody else was doing the same about us. Of course, we thought Mother was way behind the times with this saying, but now know she was much wiser than we gave her credit for at that time in our lives. I have since learned that there is "good" gossip and "bad" gossip and if we are truly living our life as God intended us to live it, we have no time for the "bad"—only the "good."

GO TO FRANCE

I never knew if my Mother was aware of how far France was from our Canadian shores, but I knew that she knew it was not around the corner. As children, whenever we got too much to handle, and that was often, Mother would say very adamantly, "GO TO FRANCE." In other words, she wanted us as far out of her sight at that particular point in time as possible. We got the message loud and clear and would quickly disappear as we knew we better not even utter a sound. We were definitely not on her good list and the results could be very negative for us.

SO HEAVENLY BOUND THAT THEY
ARE NO EARTHLY GOOD

I can't quite remember whether it was my Mother or me who came up with this saying but I clearly remember that we were on the same page in our understanding of it. There are some people in life you want to duck when you see them coming as you know you are going to receive an only "heavenly bound" lecture from them. I know my Mother believed in enjoying the many blessings God has put here on earth for His children to enjoy as long as we keep Him first in our lives. While writing this book, I ran into one such person who is as sweet as she can be, but her every word is on being "HEAVENLY BOUND" and the hereafter. I am a believer that there is a hereafter, but know that the only thing that is for sure is the present and that we are all needed to make whatever happens happen.

IT JUST WENT LIKE LOVELY

No matter what the affair was that my Mother would be attending—a shower, wedding, birthday party, church social—and she had a wonderful time, she would always say, "IT JUST WENT LIKE LOVELY." To this day, whenever my siblings and I get together, whether in person or over the telephone, and are commenting on some affair we attended, we jokingly remark, as Mother would say, "IT JUST WENT LIKE LOVELY," and we laugh.

YOU HAVE AN ENGLISH TONGUE IN YOUR HEAD—USE IT

One of the things that annoys me is when young people answer me by nodding their heads. I find myself reiterating my Mother's words, "YOU HAVE AN ENGLISH TONGUE IN YOUR HEAD—USE IT." As children, when we would mumble, usually because we were upset at something our Mother had said, Mother would emphatically say these words to us and we would straighten up and speak proper. It never ceases to amaze me the influence parents have on children, in shaping the human beings we are still becoming.

I SENT YOU TO SCHOOL TO PASS— NOT FAIL

You know how excited children get at the end of a school year when they receive their report card, which happily states that they have passed into the next grade. Well as children, my siblings and I could hardly wait for our Father to come home from work when we would greet him with "I passed, I passed" to which our Father would smile and quietly say, "I don't know what you are getting so happy about since I SENT YOU TO SCHOOL TO PASS—NOT FAIL" and we grew up with that belief that it was expected of us to pass. Furthermore, when we were growing up there was no such thing as "Summer School" and if you failed you repeated the same grade. From the first day of each school year, we knew we were expected to work hard and move forward. I believe children, as well as many adults, respond to what is expected of them.

SHE HAS ON SWAN STREET SHOES

After sailing from her home in Barbados in 1920, it took my Mother 49 years before she was able to return for a visit accompanied by some of her children. During our childhood years, we wore a lot of "hand-me-downs," including shoes. Whenever our shoes would squeak, or any one else's, our Mother would say in a joking way, "SHE HAS ON SWAN STREET SHOES." Well, during our visit with Mother to her home village, we not only had the privilege of seeing the home, school and church that were part of her beginnings, but we also went to "SWAN STREET." Shoes are still sold on "SWAN STREET" but whether or not they still squeak we'll never know. It was a very special time for us to share this childhood memory with our Mother.

YOU JUST STAND STICKY

As teenagers we often feel we know everything and truly believe parents are a little "square," especially when they lay down the law on what we can or cannot do. Then as we get older we realize they did know what they were talking about. Whenever my Mother was disappointed in something we did or did not do, she would often end up her scolding by saying, "YOU JUST STAND STICKY." She meant that if we didn't start "doing the right thing" that a year from that point in time we would be in the exact same place. I now understand what she meant. I'm so glad I decided to "move."

HE'S LIKE A SLY MONGOOSE

When one has the ability to see through people the term "Mother Wit" is often used. Well my Mother had an extra amount of this, especially when it came to young men dating her daughters. The one thing that would be in the young man's favor was if he had manners, he would immediately gain some brownie points. If, for some reason, there was something she did not particularly like about the person, she would resort to her favorite words–"HE'S LIKE A SLY MONGOOSE," which meant he could not be trusted. It was her way of warning us that he wasn't all that he pretended to be, and the irony of this was that she was usually right.

YOU ALL GO ALONG

Our parents, in raising us, always stressed the fact that no matter where we go or how many people we befriended, we should never forget the fact that family is important and deserves a special place in each of our lives. Well, to put it mildly, they did such a great job in that area, especially with their daughters, that when our Mother would try to deal with something she did not like that one of us had done, she got very little sympathy from the rest of us and would say as she threw her hands toward us, "YOU ALL GO ALONG." She would further add that she didn't know why she bothered saying anything as we were "thicker than thieves." It was and still is a beautiful feeling.

TRUE EYE SERVANT

Even though I never ever heard my Mother use the words "TRUE EYE SERVANT," my eldest brother, George, enlightened me on our Mother's great pleasure in saying them. After questioning him as to what she meant, I immediately understood what he was saying. In our lives we come across people who only work hard and can do no wrong when someone is watching, but left on their own they barely do anything. If one is only capable of working and/or performing under watch, they have not only "missed the boat," but will also miss their future.

MAKE THEM COME 'ROUND

We not only got our persistent determination from our Father, our Mother was equally strong and would not hesitate to make known how she felt when the need arose for action on her part in a troubling situation. Her favorite words at a time like this were, "MAKE THEM COME 'ROUND," which in lay terminology meant to stay on top of the situation especially when you believed you were in the right. She did not feel there was need for ugly arguments with negative results, but that we make it very clear how strongly we felt and that we should not give in until the matter was amicably resolved—even if never forgotten.

JUST BECAUSE YOU DON'T HAVE MONEY, YOU DON'T HAVE TO LOOK LIKE YOU DON'T HAVE IT

My parents were very dapper. If you saw them at a social affair, you would never know, unless you knew them personally, that they had fourteen children. The best part of this was not only did they do it for themselves; they did it for all of us. Their motto was "JUST BECAUSE YOU DON'T HAVE MONEY, YOU DON'T HAVE TO LOOK LIKE YOU DON'T HAVE IT." The fact that my Mother was an excellent seamstress was a plus as she made many of our outfits. Even though at times we wore hand-me-downs from older siblings, when it was our turn for something new, my Mother encouraged us to choose what we liked regardless of the cost and that wonderful experience in our childhood remains with all of us. To this day, if I cannot afford to buy what I really like, or find the time to make it, as I love to sew, I will do without it. It was never a question of quantity, but quality that my parents taught us by their example.

THEY DIDN'T TAKE IT LIKE IT HAS BEEN

At times in our lives we may experience "misunderstanding." It could be as a result of something someone said or something we said to someone. In either case it usually carries a disturbing feeling. When I think back on when this would happen with my Mother, she would say in her beautiful Barbadian accent, "THEY DIDN'T TAKE IT LIKE IT HAS BEEN." She would always be a little sad because what was said was definitely taken the wrong way and she would proceed to try and make it right. My Mother's sincere consideration of other people's feelings made me aware that although misunderstandings do happen, one always has the choice to try and correct the problem.

"WONNA"

Tears are filling my eyes as I am typing this most favorite word of my Mother's. If she didn't say it once a day she never said it at all. I do not even know the correct spelling as it certainly is not in the dictionary, but oh, it is such music to my ears especially when my siblings and I say it in conversation. Another beautiful remembrance of this word was when my cousin Ruby would jokingly ask Mother, "Dear Aunt (the name both of our families used when referring to our respective Aunt), how do you spell "WONNA?" Not only would my Mother shriek with laughter but so would any of us present at that particular time. Mother never gave us an answer but continued to use it whenever she was referring to family members. She never used it with outsiders and what I devise from this is that it was a special love word for family only.

YOU GIRLS BETTER FIND OUT
WHAT THEY DO BECAUSE I KNOW
THEY DO SOMETHING

My eldest sister, Kathleen, has eight children who are all now young adults, but years ago when they were younger she told our Mother that she was taking after her. My Mother became so indignant and quickly replied by saying, "how ridiculous–I didn't know any better but YOU GIRLS BETTER FIND OUT WHAT THEY DO BECAUSE I KNOW THEY DO SOMETHING." This was a giant step for our Mother to say anything regarding sex to us. She was always so relieved when we found out about puberty from friends and passed it on to each other. I'm so glad that times have changed with the majority of parents bonding with their children in this important stage of their lives.

TAKE IT WITH A GRAIN OF SALT

It's not so much what happens in our lives, what really matters is our attitude towards it. Why do we have to wait so long to get so smart about simple things? My mother used to always tell us this but only she would say, "TAKE IT WITH A GRAIN OF SALT" and we all know how small "a grain of salt" is. When you stop and really think about how ridiculous we can get over the littlest thing, we really need to kick ourselves. When we finally come to our senses, we surmise it truly was not worth all the fuss and bother.

DEAD AS A HOOK

When you enjoyed living as much as my Mother did and loved people, you sort of caught your breath whenever she made the comment, "DEAD AS A HOOK." These words out of my Mother's mouth signified that whoever or whatever she was referring to was a big disappointment. She could have been referring to a program she attended, a party she had been excited about going to, someone she met, or an event she was personally involved in. After a brief explanation of what had upset her, she would shrug her shoulders and say, "so what" and that was the end of it.

A COVER FOR EVERY POT A
PLASTER FOR EVERY SORE

One of the things I love about taking public transportation is that you meet a lot of interesting people. But even more fascinating, it affords one the opportunity of becoming a people-watcher. The people who fascinate me the most are what society would call "odd couples." I always wondered how they met and what attracted them to each other. If this happened and I was with one of my sisters, she would quickly remind me of what our Mother would say, "A COVER FOR EVERY POT A PLASTER FOR EVERY SORE." The matter was once again settled by Mother, even though she is no longer physically with us but her spirit reigns supreme.

DON'T BE FOOLISH–DO YOU THINK
I WOULD GIVE YOU MY LAST?

There was no question that our parents loved us, but even they had limits. On one of my visits home, during a period when I was experiencing some financial difficulties, my Mother gave me some money. I felt she was giving me too much and told her that I did not want to take her last dollar. She very emphatically looked at me and said, "DON'T BE FOOLISH—DO YOU THINK I WOULD GIVE YOU MY LAST?" Talk about setting me straight. I really had to chuckle at the fact that I truly had overstepped my boundaries. What a great lesson I learned from this remark.

BEGINNING IS HALF DONE

How many times in one week do you procrastinate about something you really need to do? Do you keep saying to yourself, I have just got to get those papers together and complete my report, or make that telephone call, and you keep putting it off? Welcome to the club! My Father's favorite words in such a dilemma would be, "BEGINNING IS HALF DONE." He was right on the money, because once you start doing what you have been procrastinating about, before you know it it's finished and you wonder to yourself, why did I waste so much time procrastinating about this. As I get wiser and older, I procrastinate less, do much more and end up with plus time to, of course, do something else I had been procrastinating about.

FEED THEM WITH A LONG SPOON

Anyone who really knows me knows that I love to share my busy life and thus, I love to talk. Well, I am learning that what I consider my "norm" can be a royal pain to someone on the receiving end. It has taken me a long time to put to use my Mother's advice while growing up and had difficulty handling some negative comments, especially from friends, and she would say, "FEED THEM WITH A LONG SPOON." I now do and it really works.

CAN YOU BEAT THAT?

At first glance, you might think I was talking about a competition, as we are daily inundated with everything we see, hear or read to winning. No, these words were used by my Mother to express utter disbelief in something that was either said or done by someone, which would almost take my Mother's breath away and cause her to emphatically say, "CAN YOU BEAT THAT?" Of course it never required an answer, as it was the answer.

GOD NEVER CLOSED A DOOR THAT HE DIDN'T OPEN A WINDOW

I t wasn't until we left that wonderful umbrella of our parents called "home," that we would begin to understand their further advice to us that "GOD NEVER CLOSED A DOOR THAT HE DIDN'T OPEN A WINDOW." They were so right. In my 40-year "EGO" journey I have experienced many "doors" and "windows" to last the rest of my life. The upshot of this is to know that God is so concerned about every detail of our life that when a "door" closes, He will definitely open a "window" and all we need do is take a deep breath and move forward.

FOOLISH 'TIL SOME LEFT

Have you ever tried to explain what you consider a simple thought to someone and they just don't seem to get it? The more you explain, the more complicated the matter becomes. You begin to wonder if the problem is with you in your inability to get your point across. While none of us are perfect, I find myself resorting to thinking, Mother was right, this person is "FOOLISH 'TIL SOME LEFT" which means that they are never going to really understand what you are saying as their ability to do so may be clouded or limited. You then just change the subject and move on.

THANKS, BUT I DIDN'T DIE, HE DID

I'll never forget on a visit home with my friend, Connie, shortly after my Father had passed away. Connie was expressing her sympathy to my Mother who had the habit of standing with her arms folded when conversing. My Mother kept nodding her head while listening so intently as Connie spoke and when she finished my Mother in all seriousness said to her, "THANKS, BUT I DIDN'T DIE, HE DID." I remember Connie and I laughing so hard at the serious way in which my Mother spoke as she truly believed that one should rejoice at death and cry at birth. You know over the years I have come to believe that she was absolutely right on.

HOLD THE LIGHT FOR EVEN THE DEVIL TO SEE

I'm sure that each and every one of us comes across someone who just rubs you the wrong way. It could be a family member, a boss, a co-worker, or even a friend. It seems that no matter how hard you try to do or say what you believe to be the right thing, they always find something wrong with it and to go a step further, they seem to enjoy the fact that they touched a nerve—sometimes your last nerve! My Mother always had this wonderful saying— "HOLD THE LIGHT FOR EVEN THE DEVIL TO SEE"—meaning that we should never stoop to their level but always react on a higher plain. What great advice for living, as you know life is definitely "no bed of roses."

I WONDERED WHEN YOU WERE GOING TO START USING THAT BUMP ON YOUR SHOULDER

'll never forget how excited I was when two other ladies and myself birthed "Ego Studios" (a self-improvement environment for females ages 7–77+). I could not wait to tell my family about this amazing opportunity. Also, it was something I wanted to especially tell my Father in person rather than over the telephone. With an all-knowing smile on his face, he said, "I WONDERED WHEN YOU WERE GOING TO START USING THAT BUMP ON YOUR SHOULDER." It is so wonderful when someone who truly loves you has such a vision of your abilities and believes in you. It gave me the strength and enthusiasm I needed for the journey that was set before. We need to pass this on.

IF YOU DON'T HAVE HORSE, YOU RIDE COW

The fact that you are reading this tells me that you are very tuned into life and have a sense of curiosity and have at some point experienced the need to change direction and/or method of reaching your goals. I know that I have had to take many detours and would always comment to myself one of my Mother's favorite sayings that, "IF YOU DON'T HAVE HORSE, YOU RIDE COW." While the ride on a horse, in other words, staying on course is much more enjoyable, the ride on a cow stretches you in more ways than one, with you eventually reaching your goal. I love this analogy.

IT'S ONLY A BUS STOP ON THE WAY TO WHERE YOU ARE GOING

Have you ever felt that your life was not moving in the direction or at the pace you had envisioned it would and that you felt "stuck in a rut?" I experienced such a time in my life where I was busy and involved but felt like I was going nowhere. My Father came to my rescue and enlightened me to the fact that what I was experiencing was only a "BUS STOP" in my life allowing me time to really think about my next "STOP" and whether I wanted to get off or stay on the "bus" until I reached my destination. While a simplistic explanation, it took me many years before I understood what he really meant, and I have had extreme pleasure in passing it on to so many people who have felt trapped at some point in their life. Remember, nothing is forever; therefore, you should try and enjoy the "STOP" as your arrival at your eventual destination will offer a wonderful inner peace.

IT'S NOT LOST—IT'S ONLY MISPLACED

Over the years, like most people, I have misplaced numerous items, believing at first that they were lost forever and then I would say to myself, remember what Daddy would say, "IT'S NOT LOST–IT'S ONLY MIS-PLACED." I really don't believe in magic, but most of the time, within a matter of hours, or a day, or maybe a week, whatever I had lost would re-appear. I have come to the conclusion that the expectation of finding the lost item has a lot to do with actually finding it and thus reinforces that wonderful saying of "mind over matter."

JESUS, LOVER OF MY SOUL

I'm sure most of us have had times in our lives when it seems that we are carrying the whole world on our shoulders and want to just disappear for a while. In retrospect, I think back as to what it must have been like for my parents trying to hold it all together for our family. It has taken me years to understand what my Mother may have been experiencing when she would cry out loud and clear, "JESUS, LOVER OF MY SOUL." I believe that whenever she would say these words it would strengthen her trust in God and would bring her great inner peace. How blessed we were to have this type of remembrance imprinted on our minds and nurtured in our lives.

NEVER PUT ALL YOUR EGGS IN ONE BASKET

One of my Father's ingredients for a successful life was that we be self-sufficient human beings. He truly believed it was important that we be able to make a living at doing more than one thing and doing them well. While growing up he would constantly say to us, "NEVER PUT ALL YOUR EGGS IN ONE BASKET," and even though I did not totally understand what he meant at that time, I now realize that my subconscious was digesting it all. In hindsight, I literally have put my eggs in so many baskets, which has provided me with a life journey that has been so fantastic that when I say to people that "I love my life," they always look at me in awe and often congratulate me. The wonderful thing is that "the best is yet to come" and I can hardly wait.

IT'S NOT HOW MUCH MONEY YOU MAKE SWEETHEART, IT'S WHAT YOU DO WITH WHAT YOU'VE GOT

Besides wanting to be a lawyer, my Father's other dream was to own his own home. While he did not become a lawyer, he certainly bought his first home back in the 1940's. In view of the fact that my Father never earned $100.00 per week during his lifetime, had a wife and 14 children, it was an honorable accomplishment. I honestly thought we were rich, but in hindsight I remember my Father always saying, "IT'S NOT HOW MUCH MONEY YOU MAKE SWEETHEART, IT'S WHAT YOU DO WITH WHAT YOU'VE GOT." Further, he added that all through our lives we will be making choices and that while we may feel the need to earn more money (not that there is anything wrong with that thinking), we need to pay more attention to how we handle the money we have. At this stage in my life, I am totally understanding what he meant. Better late than never.

FULL OF AIR SAUCE AND WIND PUDDING

This saying, "FULL OF AIR SAUCE AND WIND PUDDING" originally came from my sister, Gerri, but my Mother loved it so much that she constantly used it—especially when describing someone who had great difficulty in telling the truth. She would comment on the fact that said person did it so often they actually believed what they were saying was the truth. In other words, they were a habitual liar. I'm sure at some point in your life you have come across such a person. I have, and while the person may be funny in their deliverance of the "lie," I consider it an insult to my intelligence. My main concern in this regard is what happens if and when said person is actually telling the truth and you don't believe them. Then this is sad!

HASTE MAKES WASTE

Even though we know that "HASTE MAKES WASTE" we still find ourselves rushing about like there is no tomorrow. I've often wondered if the "rushing" I'm experiencing is due to the fact that I am getting older and trying to keep pace with my busy life, or whether I feel the need to hurry because that's basically my nature. I do believe that I am finally at the point where I know Mother knew best when she would say "HASTE MAKES WASTE" as each time I find myself really pushing too hard, I lean back, take a deep breath and just slow down. I find I accomplish just as much, if not more, and certainly it keeps my stress level at a minimum.

TOO FINEY, FINEY

I'm truly chuckling as I am typing this due to the fact that the whole world is consumed with their body image and in many ways I know that is a good place to be. You see a great part of my business has to do with not only feeling emotionally good about one's self, but looking physically together. Despite this fact, I have never wanted to nor could I be "thin" due to my bone structure. I'll go a step further and put the blame on my Mother who would comment when someone was very thin that they looked "TOO FINEY, FINEY," adding that they had no front and no back and looked more like an ironing board. We would laugh, but comments like that stick with you—especially coming from your Mother.

HOWEVER YOU MAKE YOUR BED, YOU LIE IN IT

Nobody loved weddings more than my Mother, especially if the wedding was one of her daughter's. She thoroughly enjoyed being the Mother of the Bride in every sense of the word, but possessed one very redeeming quality—she never ever interfered in any of our lives. Her great advice to each of us was always the same, "HOWEVER YOU MAKE YOUR BED, YOU LIE IN IT." Whenever our parents heard us complain about our personal lives, they never took sides but would just advise us to try and work things out, and the way they said it, we knew the conversation was over. I now know they were very wise in their decision.

HEY, I FALL OFF TO NOTHING

With our nation obsessed with losing weight, or at least some of us should be, I get so tickled remembering my Mother and her friends when they would be talking about gaining or losing weight. In the latter instance, they all would say the same thing, "HEY, I FALL OFF TO NOTHING," which literally meant that they had lost some weight. Can you just picture our weight-conscious, anti-aging society of the 21st century using such words? I do not know if this was a West Indian saying, but it certainly was their way of expressing weight loss. It was never interpreted in pounds, inches or dress size. They certainly were not members of a gym or a weight loss club, but they did walk almost everywhere. The one thing I knew that most of them did was cut back on what they put into their bodies. Does this ring a bell? It seems that is exactly where we are—intake and exercise. Good, old-fashioned common sense.

GOD NEVER GIVES YOU MORE
THAN YOU CAN BEAR

At the time of writing this book, I am completing what has been the busiest yet most rewarding year of my life. Each time something new and of special interest to me would come along, I would say to myself, "Well I believe God has sent this so He must believe that I can do it." At times when I felt overwhelmed, I would recall what Mother would say, "GOD NEVER GIVES YOU MORE THAN YOU CAN BEAR." I question this statement, as I also know that God has given us the freedom of choice and maybe I was making too many "yes" choices and in some instances only able to deliver "no" results. The only way I have been able to balance my life has been through prayer. I highly recommend it.

RICHNESS IS NOT IN YOUR POCKET
IT'S IN YOUR THINKING

It wasn't until I read Napoleon Hill's book *THINK AND GROW RICH* did I begin to understand a statement my Father shared with me years ago. He said that many people enjoyed bragging about how rich they were and would proceed to pull out their wallets to prove their lot. He said never be swayed by this action, as real richness was in our thinking. How we felt about ourselves, about our fellow-man and how we lived our lives was the true measure of richness. He stressed the importance of doing and giving our best no matter the situation and would add that we, his children, were his legacy to the world.

SHE JUST LOOKED LIKE A DONE OUT OLD SOUL

As I am typing this page, I have this wonderful vision of my Mother when she would say with sincere feeling, "SHE JUST LOOKED LIKE A DONE OUT OLD SOUL." Whenever she said these words it was always with great love and had little bearing on the age of the person. We all know that life can be tough and at times one is not able to bounce back and sometimes the struggle can wear you down—not only inwardly but outwardly as well. Should my path cross someone who appeared this way, I would immediately remember my Mother's words and be thankful for my many blessings.

THE WATCHED POT NEVER BOILS

I'm sure most of us have experienced how impatient we become when waiting for a phone call, a letter, a doctor's report, or even a pot to boil. When I was growing up and would hear my Mother say, "THE WATCHED POT NEVER BOILS," I always thought she was referring to something she was cooking even though at that point in time she actually was not cooking. Now I understand she was referring to life because the moment our conscience lets go and becomes attuned to something totally different, even for a second, whatever we were anxiously waiting for happens. I now realize that I was being given another lesson for living.

IF HE KNEW BETTER
HE WOULD DO BETTER

One Sunday morning, I heard one of my favorite men of God emphatically say that often we criticize someone unfairly when we do not know all the facts. At certain times in my life I can plead guilty to this statement. This man of God continued, in essence, by saying, "Did you for one moment think about the fact that IF HE KNEW BETTER HE WOULD DO BETTER." I thought of how often my Mother would say these very same words when unfair comments were being made about someone or a situation—especially when the comments came from her children.

SHE NEEDS LICKS

We all make mistakes, but making the same mistake over and over would have caused my Mother to say, "SHE NEEDS LICKS." Being so strong mentally, emotionally and physically as my Mother was, she could not understand anyone being a doormat for someone else, regardless of whether it was a spouse, children, parents or friends. She had such a strong sense of self and would always lecture us in this regard. I think one of the many things I admired most about my Mother was that she was always open to learn something new and got so excited each time life handed her the opportunity.

JOSEPH OF MANY COLORS

There is no doubt that we need to laugh more in our lives as most everything today is so serious and on a fast track. I know that laughter was a big part of our family life, as my parents would always see the humor in almost everything. I should mention the fact that my Mother was always fashion coordinated so when she would make a comment to the effect that someone looked like "JOSEPH OF MANY COLORS" we knew exactly what she was saying. There was no harm intended by my Mother as all it did was provide a shared moment of laughter with no one's feelings being hurt.

IF YOU DON'T LAUGH, YOU'LL CRY

The longer you live, the more you realize that life is no bed of roses. It can hand you some tough places to hoe. You experience many things that are bittersweet in life when you really want to cry but decide to laugh. I'm convinced that my Mother believed this, as she would comment after a troubling situation or on hearing some disturbing news, "IF YOU DON'T LAUGH, YOU'LL CRY." You guessed it—she always laughed. I loved her spirit.

I'M NOT READY YET

My Father died in his 83rd year and my Mother lived for 24 years following his death. There is no mystery to this, just the simple fact that my Mother was 13 years younger than my Father. As friends would pass away, Mother would feel a sense of sadness but always followed it up with her famous words, "I know that I have to go one day, but I'M NOT READY YET." She was determined to stay around as long as she could and did so by keeping pace traveling with her daughters and in some instances would outpace us by traveling on her own. I truly believe she extended her life with her constant affirmation of "I'M NOT READY YET." When it was time for Mother to go, she was ready.

NO MATTER HOW THE CORN SELLS

I f you love corn on the cob like I do, whether in or out of season, I don't care what it costs I am going to buy it. This is the rationale my Mother used when she made up her mind to do or get something she really wanted and inevitably would say, "NO MATTER HOW THE CORN SELLS, I'm going to do it." Most of the time "it" was something she either wanted for our home, or for one of her children. If the latter, especially if it was your turn for something new instead of a hand-me-down, my Mother would move heaven and earth to accomplish this feat. It was exciting to see her in action and each of us inherited this strong trait from her, which truly has benefited our lives and others.

OH, FOR LAND SAKE

The other day after someone had relayed some disturbing information to me, I quickly responded, "OH, FOR LAND SAKE" to which the person giving the information asked, "What was that you just said?" I replied, "Oh, it was something my Mother would always say when she heard some upsetting news." To this day, I don't really know what she truly meant when she said this, and at this point in time in my life, it really doesn't matter. It only affirms to me an old adage—"that the apple doesn't fall too far from the tree."

STILL PUSHING

In this hi-tech NOW world in which we are constantly navigating our lives, I find that I just get sick and tired of all the deadlines in which I find myself. Every now and then I ask myself, "Why am I doing this?" And I keep getting the same answer - because I want to and usually enjoy what it is I am doing. To go a step further, I truly believe I inherited my zest for living from my parents. Whenever I stop a minute and take a deep breath, I can almost hear my Mother saying, "STILL PUSHING." This was a constant response to any one of her children whenever we asked her how she was doing, whether in person or over the telephone. And "PUSH" she did for almost 94 years. Her love of life was contagious and I'm so glad I received a heavy dose.

TO BE SURE

I am sure you have heard the words "TO BE SURE" somewhere along life's journey. I have heard it said as a firm statement and I have also heard it said as a question. Of course, my Mother's version was a firm statement with no ifs, ands, or buts. I have come to the conclusion that it can be used whenever and however one wishes. I have always taken it as a positive and it has served me well. The choice is yours.

YOU CAN BE STILL AND MAKE A BIG NOISE

Have you ever had the experience of making a positive impression on people without ever saying one word? This has happened to me on a few occasions at which time it would remind me of something my Father said during one of our wonderful conversations. "Sweetheart, you know YOU CAN BE STILL AND MAKE A BIG NOISE," and he was absolutely right. My first such experience was in a Church I visited and subsequently joined. Several times it has happened at schools where I was presenting lessons from our "EGO" program on self-awareness and self-esteem. Another time it happened was when a young lady followed me off a bus to let me know how safe she always felt once she saw that I, too, was on the same bus during a period we were both working late. Boy, talk about making my day—she did!

WORRY IS DEBT PAID BEFORE IT BECOMES DUE

I believe that at times in our life we worry endlessly about something which never happens and wonder why we did that. My Father always said to us that, "WORRY IS DEBT PAID BEFORE IT BECOMES DUE," and would allude to the fact that while there is nothing wrong in being concerned about something of importance that was taking place in our life, but to let it consume a majority of one's thoughts was not healthy. My own experience has proven to me that excessive concentration on a problem tends to magnify it resulting in a heavy dose of stress and too little sleep. Once I rationalized that I was my own worst enemy and mistreating my body, I re-arranged my priorities with very positive results.

TIRED . . . I'M PAST TIRED

Have you ever felt so tired that you just couldn't take another step if your life depended on it? You don't want to eat, you don't want to talk and in some instances you can't even sleep. Speaking from my own personal experience it is a sin to do this to one's self, but I have been guilty of this on more than one occasion. It is a horrible feeling and the solution for me is to just be still. The one thing that crosses my mind during a time like this and usually conjures up a smile is remembering when my Mother used to say, "TIRED . . . I'M PAST TIRED," as I can truly relate.

TWO HEADS ARE BETTER
THAN ONE

One day I was busy pricing items for a table display at a Luncheon and making sure they were easy to read and thus placed them across the tops of the various items. Upon completion of this very tedious job, I was definitely not pleased with the overall outcome and knew I could do a better job, but at that moment I was coming up blank to what should have been a very simple solution. I quickly telephoned my sister, Doris, who lives in Toronto, explained my dilemma to which she immediately responded, "Place them on the bottom." I said thanks, hung up the phone, and smilingly acknowledged one of my Father's favorite statements, "TWO HEADS ARE BETTER THAN ONE," especially when the mind is open to receive.

YOU CATCH MORE BEES WITH HONEY

Many of you reading this have experienced the frustration at some time in your life of not having enough money to pay your bills coupled with the constant attention one might receive from creditors. It can become a bit overwhelming and I can speak with some authority in this regard as at the time of this writing I am just beginning to catch my breath from a horrendous period of dealing with creditors in an effort to hang on to my business. Some of them would be very human while others were absolutely obnoxious. One day after a negative experience, my conscience was penetrated by one of my Father's favorite sayings, "YOU CATCH MORE BEES WITH HONEY SWEETHEART," and started doing just that which not only relieved me of the frustration I felt towards the creditors, who were only doing their job, but at the same time resulted in a very positive response, respect and assistance from these same callers. This experience reaffirmed the fact that we are never too old to learn.

THERE IS NOTHING WRONG WITH WHAT YOU ARE DOING, THE ONLY THING THAT IS WRONG, IS YOU

In 1967, the year my dear Father passed away, we were having one of our many in-depth conversations in which I was expressing what I was feeling at that time—my inability to make a real "go" of my business, "Ego Studios." You should know that at the beginning of 1967 our "Ego" partnership dissolved and I decided to operate "Ego" on my own. As confident as I usually feel about my decisions, I was experiencing serious doubts. My Father listened and then said, "THERE IS NOTHING WRONG WITH WHAT YOU ARE DOING, THE ONLY THING THAT IS WRONG IS YOU." I quickly responded with great exclamation "Me!" My Father replied, "Knowing you like I do, you would never be at peace with yourself if you quit now—you would always be questioning yourself as to what you could have or should have done. Give yourself a chance. I believe you will find out things about yourself which might never happen if you give up now." I'm so glad I listened and stayed on course.

YOU ONLY PASS THIS WAY ONE TIME

When I stop and catch my breath realizing we are about to celebrate the 40ᵗʰ Anniversary of "Ego Studios," I am blown away with how fast time passes when you're living your life to its fullest. Even in the most difficult of times when I just wanted to do absolutely nothing, I would force myself to do at least one positive thing, even if it was scrubbing a floor, as I could still hear in the recesses of my mind my Mother who would always say to us, "YOU ONLY PASS THIS WAY ONE TIME" and we better make the best of it as there was no coming back. When you are gone you are gone—but not my Mother—she is still spiritually here.

FREE, SINGLE AND DISENGAGED AND NOT TAKING CARE OF ANOTHER LIVING SOUL

A couple of years after our Father died, we were teasing our Mother about the possibility that she might marry again, even though we truly believed it was definitely not on her agenda. She was at the time living alone and seemed to be enjoying the "empty nest" syndrome—some of us married and others living on their own. Our Mother emphatically took this opportunity to set the record straight by telling us she loved being "FREE, SINGLE AND DISENGAGED" and that she was "NOT TAKING CARE OF ANOTHER LIVING SOUL." Could you honestly blame her after raising all of us and then taking care of her husband during the latter years of his life when his health weakened? You can believe we got her message and never again broached the subject.

NO TRUE MEMBER

After 40 years of living and servicing my dream, "Ego Studios," I can truly relate to one of my Mother's favorite "sayings" when she was disappointed with the action of someone and would comment that the person involved was "NO TRUE MEMBER." It took me a long time to realize that there are some people who just "talk the talk" to hear themselves but never "walk the walk." As one who has always tried my best to be a person of my word, no matter what arena I was working in, I still find it difficult to totally accept from some people what I believe to be a sincere interest and/or comment and find myself thinking, "I better not count on that" as past behavior is a sure sign that they definitely fall into the category of "NO TRUE MEMBER." Trust is something that is earned no matter if you are giving or receiving and the former is the better.

NEVER A WEARY MORNING

When I get excited about something I want to do—for instance this tribute to my parents—I can hardly wait for morning to come. Although I love the sunshine, dreary weather usually never squelches my enthusiasm as to what surprises the new day has in store, even if some days feed you more negatives than positives. My Mother demonstrated this way of living every day of her life, reinforcing her beliefs with sayings so lovingly stored in my memory bank such as, "NEVER A WEARY MORNING." When I hear these words in my subconscious, I remember how passionate my Mother felt about life—so much so that each and every morning to her was a gift and therefore "never weary."

IF YOU THINK TRYING IS RISKY WAIT 'TIL YOU GET THE BILL FOR NOT TRYING

The above "saying" came from my sister, Mary, and I felt it was perfect for the next-to-last "saying" in this book. My solid upbringing provided the foundation for me to follow my dreams even when they did not make sense to others. The biggest risk was my decision, along with two other ladies, to birth "Ego Studios" over 40 years ago and I'm so thankful we did. The journey, though bumpy at times, has been challenging allowing me to grow in many directions and offered a unique opportunity to touch and change lives in a positive way. Remember God has designed a plan for each one of us. All we have to do is allow Him in our lives, step out in faith and enjoy the ride. I'm so glad I did as I truly believe and constantly say, "The best is yet to come."

COMMENCEMENT

My Father would be so pleased to hear me say "COMMENCEMENT" which means "Beginning" as most people connect this word to be the end of a period in one's life. It's not! In fact, at the time of this writing, June 2004, the air is full of many things that are coming to fruition, such as, weddings, graduations, "Ego's" 40th Anniversary Celebration, and the completion of this book. The effort given to all these preparations while bringing them to an end really is opening them to a new beginning. In other words, to a "COMMENCEMENT."

Contact Edith Carter Johnson at
edithjohnson1103@aol.com

or order more copies of this book at:

Tate Publishing, LLC

127 East Trade Center Terrace
Mustang, Oklahoma 73064

(888) 361 - 9473

Tate Publishing, Llc